OH SHENANDOAH!

David Boyle has been writing about new ideas for more than a quarter of a century. He is co-director of the New Weather Institute, policy director of Radix UK, a fellow of the New Economics Foundation, has stood for Parliament and is a former independent reviewer for the Cabinet Office. He is the author of *Tickbox, Alan Turing, Scandal* and *Before Enigma*, as well as a range of other books and stories, including the Caractacus trilogy. He lives in the South Downs.

Oh, Shenandoah!

and other poems

David Boyle

THE REAL PRESS

www.therealpress.co,uk

Published in 2021 by the Real Press.
www.therealpress.co.uk © David Boyle

ISBN (print) 9781912119011
ISBN (ebks)   9781912119226

Cover picture by Sarah Burns
(www.sarahburnspatterns.com)

For my wonderful boys, Robin and William Boyle,
with love.

Contents

Introduction

There is a kind of progression here, but I didn't want to jinx it by trying to describe it. Either way, many of these poems were written in my thirties – hence the 'Thirtysomething' title taken from the television series of the same name and time.

A small piece of nostalgia there...

'Oh Shenandoah' was intended as a kind of rhetorical acceleration. I had the idea waiting outside the only shower room on a Writing Space writing course in the Loire Valley and listening to someone inside singing the old Shenandoah song.

That was my first published poem, which managed to scrape in as a finalist and runner-up in the national Observer-Arvon poetry competition in 1995.

In fact, this and so much else I owe to Carol Cornish and Writing Space, under whose tutelage so many of these poems took their first faltering steps.

I stopped writing poetry almost entirely about a decade later, when – having had children – I suddenly had no time to mooch around in the way that poets need to.

I hope to go back to the practice one day, when I also hope I feel a little differently to the somewhat obsessive type revealed in these pages.

David Boyle
Steyning, Christmas 2021

Oh, Shenandoah!

Oh, Shenandoah,
 I love your daughter.
And though I felt comfortable,
loving even, with so many others,
I find I can no longer continue
my life as an actuary and clerk
in a middle-sized firm of city insurance brokers
without her devotion,
love, passion, desire, thrill, excitement,
hand across the table on a cold winter evening,
unwashed face across the pillow in the morning.
I love your daughter
and the earth turned on its axis when I did so,
and whole seasons have shifted around the globe,
the ocean has swallowed up New York, Sydney, Tokyo,
and caused a run on the pound,
the British Chancellor has resigned and the stars have altered
    their paths.
And I can't wake without thinking of her,
can't buy a ticket at the station without thinking of her,
can't dream without thinking of her.
I am a small man, barely average height;
my prospects are unexciting to say the least
I readily admit
that a small Lambeth council tax payer has little to offer

to the daughter of one of the greatest rivers on earth,
that you and she will course your ways without me.
And yet -
what I feel is simple and seismic
about the way she throws her head back at my feeble jokes
about the way she tentatively strokes my hand
about her pink woollen socks and strange taste in wallpaper,
may lift me up beyond the crass banality of commuting.
And I will shrivel and die without her.
So give me this chance
Restore the earth
Let the ants work again, the bees sting, the cows smile, the
    beer taste, and sunlight dapple and the valleys hum
And restore me too.
Let me, for one moment, roar down the earth inexorably
    towards the sea.
Give me your strength
And let me win
And let me never forget it.

I

Thirtysomething

Thirtysomething

and every moon that rose and wained and waxed,
and every line still there when we're relaxed,
and every hopeful number filofaxed,
and every doubt, and every painful crack,
and every bruise that's left its mark in black,
and stressful, fractured bend that won't bend back
the way it used to be. And every scar,
and every sumptuous fatty meal too far,
and all that wondering who and why you are -
to keep the promise or to break the vow.
And every nuclear test our bones allow,
and every furrowed artery and brow,
and every misspent night of love gone by,
and every memory that hurts. And every lie,
and every wasted egg and sperm and cry,
and every answer or solution blurred,
and every sorry little tale we heard,
and every hope we shelved or just deferred.
Another year, another spring, has flung
us up life's ladder, slowly, rung on rung.

AND YET WE'RE STILL SO YOUNG!

Daffodils

They shone in my hands, my daffodils:
clutched bare in my palms without paper,
with innocent yellow faces
gleaming like babies
shivering with anticipation,
excited to be outside when spring is brand new,
and the sunshine watches over the street
for the first time since September.

They set my bus alight, my daffodils:
old crochety ladies, staring ahead,
beamed up at me as I fumbled for the bell,
recognition in their faces
collusion in their eyes,
because they know these flowers are evidence
of a fond romantic gift for someone
whose face also glows with the spring.

Actually I bought them myself.
They sit here now beside me on the desk,
persuading me I'm not alone.

Lost

Thirty-eight years; the things I've lost.
A large number of different coloured socks.
A whole room full of biros.
Enough pins to fill a couple of haystacks.
My youth, my unlined face,
my virginity.
My favourite book of poems by William Blake,
lost on a number 2 bus at Baker Street
along with three sandwiches.
Half a chapter on my computer when the lead fell out.
My innocence and naivety perhaps.
My blue anorak, a whole flock
of black umbrellas.
My close intimate infantile relationship with my mother.
A little bit of weight since July.
A clutch of smiling fuzzy girlfriends.
Enough hopes and causes to repopulate Oxford.
And one passionate, flawed, soft and glowing
love, mislaid somewhere across the Atlantic, and
try as I might,
though I scour my life like the woman with the lost coin,
I simply cannot lay my hands on her again.

But the universe recycles all its energy, so
maybe I'll find them all again

waiting for me
in the hereafter.

Museum Street

Still soft, like a sheepskin,
the pavement in the morning,
and a pale light bathes the street
like an open fridge.
Soapsuds from grey encrusted pails
move slowly past me:
I sit stiff by the steering wheel
waiting for 8.30 and
the meter, and traffic noise to
reach me, and breakfast
by the British Museum.
And news and love maybe.
I've been away too long:
our sleep still loiters under eyelids
the dreams still hold on tight. Through this
the tiny teapot waits for me, and
the smell of brown bacon and
individually suppressed strands of lust.

I must, I must
approach this early morning kiss with trust.

The Nut Tree

The King of Spain's daughter came,
With her black ringlets and hungry eyes,
And opened her dark lids into my face.
I loved her for her olive skin
And counted it above her jewels.
I thought she wanted me.
I showed her my silver nutmeg;
She took out her calculator.
I showed her my golden pear;
She called her broker.
And while the wind whistled through the branches
And the days slipped by like a fox in the night,
I waited for the nut tree.
The precious metals I could do without:
I just wanted the fruit, an ordinary
Apple here, a walnut there.
She brought no love, but lavished shares on me
And all for the sake of my little nut tree.

My place

Oh Pleiades, oh Milky Way,
remember my small dreams by day.
And while you shift tremendous light,
plant more majestic dreams by night.

Beyond our billion small events,
see through my insignificance,
from distant pole to distant pole,
plant your deep echo in my soul.

Oh Sirius, call out my name,
across millennia the same,
and send me starlight while I grope
to rest in joy not tinged with hope.

Burn up delusions. Burn out pain,
and let me master life again -
but life that's filled, no, not with lies,
but daily, innocent surprise.

Oh Hyades, Oh Betelgeuse,
don't let my tininess reduce
the glory of each pinprick light.
Oh Great Bear, stay there through the night.

II

The edges of things

Dark

Rage, rage against the dying of the dark.
Resist the dawn. Cheer on the gathering gloom,
And deep inside that blanket, send me dreams –

Send me down where unmade poems live,
like ancient river monsters nibbling in the deep,
green with age and meaning; where the wild things are.

Send me to the cellar, to the woods at dusk,
the feel of frost on face, the chance of magic,
To sense the dark creative roots of life.

Not every day, perhaps. But let me keep
the weedy pathway to that secret garden
well-trodden; at least the possibility of night.

So when you watch the last blue streaks of day,
the clouds of dusk beyond like great black hills
over London – don't mourn the loss of bright.

Don't mourn the roar of 4-star, DJs, DVDs,
the glass-walled fluorescent cacophony of day,
those walkmen, binaries that never sleep.

Turn off the lamp a moment, let the black

seep into the pores and know the fear,
the joy, the wealth of practising for death.

II

Sometimes the light becomes
too heavy. With its jingles
and its neon borings into minds,
and I long for darkness,
long for black so deep and fathomful
that only the stars can pierce inside.

So when the museum is closed,
the fridge door shut, the caretaker having
locked his gate and pottered home to bed,

then give me the windswept dark –
the rabbit hole abandoned on the moors
before the Wars of the Roses.

Give me the silent dark,
beyond *Titanic* on the ocean floor,
where eyeless fish just breathe and sleep.

Give me a place with the dark things, in
the deepest chapter of the night,
where the mould considers its position.

20

Where the magic sparks, with a flash
of deeper darkness. Healing happens.
Where we dream of long-forgotten things

in half-forgotten sunlight, of hopes
we never named. Where poems grow
in damp and dark and desolation.

Where I go, perhaps, to sleep and feel
a quietness in the marrow of my life and
hear the merest rumoured glimpse of God.

The edge

I am changing into something else,
And I don't mean my clothes. My skin
Bubbles like Vesuvius. I can hear
Eruptions in my colon and drumbeats in my soul.

Nobody believes me, though they sympathise.
They have seen my sick note, signed my
Sheafs of prescription. My wife smiles
And holds my hands as I lie awake.

Already there is a gauze between me
And the others in the street. I know
I couldn't reach them, move them, kiss them
If I tried. And I wait fearfully

But with a little hope, to see what I become.
Whether lizard or swan, or monstrous outsider
Caught between two bitter universes.

I just hope it's me.

The Snake

I saw a snake beside me on the road,
High on a mountain track –
Both of us some way from home perhaps,
The V for vicious branded on his head.
I'd never seen a viper before then –
Barely seen a snake except when separated
By antiseptic zoological glass.
But yes, I knew it then:
When I was young I dreaded them
Beyond the usual horrors of monstrous ghosts,
Refused to venture down the thrilling path
Where garden and brick wall met in heaps of grass,
For fear that V that lurked there would leap
Into reality. It never did,
But now we meet,
An echo through the decades
Of that dread V,
That not quite dead nightmare of the undergrowth.
But now I see it, warming in the sun,
I recognise something in it:
A fellow being far from home
Like me, an uncertain right
To be there on the road,
So flagrant in its contempt for traffic.

23

I stood above it for a moment,
My childhood fears shrunk to a proper size,
Then I looked a little closer.
It was dead.
And I felt a burst of loss,
Not for the snake perhaps, or its fear, but
For all the giant colours of childhood –
The monster of the grass,
The grandeur of life beyond the flowerbed,
Where vipers lay in wait.

Metamorphosis

My dog is brown
And lashes through the fields
Like a laugh escaping from a schoolboy.
He doesn't talk of money or joke or
Sit examinations in the gym.

But at night I dream
We're walking down Regent's Street,
Arm and arm,
Chatting about dating etiquette,
And dismantling the latest episode
Of Big Brother.

My dog smells a little
And sleeps neatly curled in a circle
Like a snake swallowing its tail.
He never gets cross or
Worries about his credit card account.

But at night I dream
We're in front of the fire at
The Railway Arms,
With our pints and packets of crisps,
Watching the barmaids
With our feet up.

My dog is dead and gone.
I loved him for his humour
And the way his ears betrayed his mood.
He never stayed angry
With me or bitter.

But at night I dream
I shake his hand and admire
His jeans and sneakers, and
Talk to him through the evening
About mystery and dying and
The shape of souls.

Tough on terror. 2003

"Ah, Bach!"
The Secretary of State exhales back in his chair,
Chords echo through his stale conditioned air
And flow on out into the dark.
The whisky next to him, and open at his side
Reports of outrages and innocence, and within reach
The corrected draft of one more 9/11 speech,
Condemning butchery, infanticide.
"If they underestimate us, they're in error ...
There are no depths to which they will not sink,"
No hint of doubt about that smile, that drink.
"We will extend our fight with terror."

His conscience shelves, becalmed by Bach,
The children blown to fragments in Iraq.

The edges of things

It's hard to brush into corners.
The detritus of time
just stays there, musing
about what might have been.

The boundaries of floors,
where the vertical
Meets the horizontal
hug their fag-butts to themselves.

**

We head for the corners
like homing lemmings –
to the seedy, the forgotten,
the edges of things.

Hoping for what? A glimpse
of other worlds perhaps,
truer, passionate worlds.
Underworlds of real life.

**

We crawl like babies
to the desert, the cliff edge,
where the seas pour away
into space-time, musing

about what might be.
The edges of things where
we hang around, and hope
to meet infinity face to face.

Afterword

Bachelor

The night pulsates with sounds you never hear.
They come wafting to me; I taste them on the air;
I feel them ripple down my spine, like
Beethoven playing the piano.
They invade my mind like the street light invades my room.
I feel them one by one, the sounds
of TV channels beating on the roof,
of money sloshing down the wires,
of palpitating adultery on the breeze,
of yearning loves which dare not be,
of stockbrokers asleep dreaming of unicorns,
of abandoned husbands weeping in the park,
of wheezing policemen hurtling towards retirement
of pacemakers like crickets, and
worms taking the long way home.

For me, the bachelor,
with neither vows nor ties,
I hear my small child weeping in the dark,
unborn, unimagined until now.
He calls out to me in the lonely parts of night
and I ache to comfort him into existence.

The Real Press

Poetry without boundaries

You can see our full range of books here a
www.therealpress.co.uk

34